Velocity of Slugs

Velocity of Slugs

Joey Connelly

Etchings Press
Indianapolis, Indiana

Copyright © 2015 by Joey Connelly

This publication is made possible by funding provided by
the College of Arts and Sciences and the English Department
at the University of Indianapolis. Special thanks to Ingram Spark,
and to the students who judged, designed, and edited this chapbook:
Tierney Bailey, Mikaela Bielawski, Rachel Holtzclaw, Alyssa Kauffman,
Adam Kuhn, Zach Lee, Dani McCormick, Rachael Neawedde, Mirna
Palacio Ornelas, and Jessi Tillman.

UNIVERSITY *of*
INDIANAPOLIS.

Published by Etchings Press
1400 E. Hanna Ave.
Indianapolis, Indiana 46227
All rights reserved

etchings.uindy.edu
www.uindy.edu/cas/english

Printed by Ingram Spark

Published in the United States of America

ISBN 978-0-9903475-1-4

22 21 20 19 18 17 16 15   2 3 4
Second Printing, 2019

Table of Contents

Self Portrait as the Holy Family 1
Cellist Writes Poems 2
Debris 3
The Day I Came Out to My Parents 4
The Lighthouse 5
Context 7
Velocity of Slugs 8
The Florist 11
Resume of the Prophet 13
Bost to Tarshish 15
Jonah Descending 16
The Listening 18
The Violation and the Laughter 22
My Own Midwife 24
Gethsemane, Kentucky 27

Acknowledgments 28

Self-Portrait as the Holy Family

Another failed prophesy, another
missed chance for closure.
The night my father, while playing poker with his brothers,
all drunk as soothsayers,
bet his only son's only bicycle,
my mom and I stayed on the porch until the sun rose,
squeaking my puppy's favorite toy,
    hoping he would come back to me.
Neighborhood boys who would never talk to me
rode menacing circles.

People love an apocalypse.
Fire, brimstone, final
surprises, funnel cakes of fire,
third generation napalm, a rape in an alley, a little
person shot from a canon.
There is no hope in an empty tomb,
only negative capability
and my ability
to see myself in a manger,
though I was born in the fanciest
of hospitals.

A Cellist Writes Poems

for Daniel

Bare page like a slashed cheek
or the first time a mouth ran down your body and the mouth
belonged to someone of your own gender

and it occurred to you then
as quick as an orgasm
that few things worth having
do not burn—
you thought of your skull and pelvis,
how the cremator must bash them with a baseball bat
after the rest of you is ashes

and outside the window the most glorious streetlight
shone just enough to make shadows of falling snow
and you watched the shadows against the streetlight
as his hot breath wormed ever downward.

Your eyes focused outside;
you accepted passive pleasure, pretending
the wealth of energy was beyond your transcendental silence.

Debris

Shame was so present then,
that summer of setting, cutting,

hanging the tobacco.
Sunburns, dirty fingernails, the sweat

all primed me for different activities.
The humid silence of barn rafters

was not enough to quiet my body,
demanding what it should not.

The turned earth gave way;
crickets clung to us briefly.

Still I knew I would always and never be more than flesh.

The Day I Came Out to My Parents

Straddling the back of the tractor, I place
tobacco sprouts into a dirty, metallic hand,
a farming relay,
and the hand pierces the dirt before revolving back
for another plant.

If I could tell a story with the earth I would,
a seamstress who uses no needles,
a potter whose hands never touch clay.
But the dirt only takes green shoots
and the sweat makes me a liar.

I smear mud on the back of my neck
for relief from the sun and realize
flesh is useless.
Hands can feel no lasting feeling.

Farm machines, like me, finish filling one line
and immediately begin another.
I ignore my steaming skin as I silently compose,
trying to be fog—almost invisible but not quite—
pretending this field is not pliant soil
but instead a place I love.

The Lighthouse

I dream sometimes of a lighthouse guarding a silver sea.
Inside I am protected by tides
and deceptive undertow.

I more often dream that I stand outside,
waves of a thousand naked corpses
smashing face down on the stones.

I search for a blanket to cover them.
The lookout window torchlit
and I can't find the door.

Worse still are the dreams where
I stand on top of the light,
clothes bloodstained,

the sky a sheet of foil
and as the light revolves
I see my reflection from every angle.

In my hand a knife and at my feet
a bruised 21 year old.
I am Abraham and I am Isaac with no angel in sight.

On the hardest nights, elements combine,
nightmarish variation on a nightmare theme.
I look down and see the dead.

I look up to see only myself in the mirrored sky
and I must either stare into my own eyes and see the blood-
    splattered knife
or turn away to face the darkness

behind darkness
and darkness
beyond still.

Context

    Breathing only produces more breathing,
a curse to throw at all I worshipped.

I bled for days from a place I could not see, where my body could not numb.
Stained the driver's seat of the car I kept long after
the drive ended.
Why admit this?
I say this as context. I say this as foreshadowing.

I am not Jonah. I do not aspire so high.
God never spoke to me. I never avoided preaching in the city of Nineveh
by sailing to Tarshish. God sent no great fish to swallow me.
I never behaved like a spoiled child,
and God never killed my plant to teach me a lesson.

Instead, my story is a bruised apple. A day at the cemetery.
Stained glass mosaic of Vietnam on flammable satin.
Feather duster of razor blades.

Velocity of Slugs

"There are only two ways by which men can deal with one another: guns or logic."
Ayn Rand

i.

I remember so little.
The after-image of a camera's flash,
moments with my entire field of vision
reduced to a purple cloud
swimming with voices.
Even those I don't remember.
There is no self-doubt like the inability to recall.

ii.

In a handgun owner's manual, they graph pressure over time
and attach words like *initial ballistics*
to make a bullet in a barrel
sound more beautiful.
Mechanics of guns a mathematical enterprise,
cold calculations of engineering and *controlled expansion of gases*
from burning gunpowder generates pressure
(force/area).

Pressure. Force. Language conveying meaning.
The graph of pressure over time looks impotent,

an inverted parabola, an upside down u.
The more time goes by, the less pressure
in a gun's chamber. Outside a gun

the opposite is true.

iii.

Kinetic energy equals half of the mass
times the squared velocity.
Velocity. What a lovely word. Velocity contains city as theodicy
   contains odyssey.

The math loses me as I ponder words involved,
because logic will never help me understand,
remember.

The connection between coefficient
and *forward motion of the bullet is also affected by drag*
which states the obvious. What a drag
and dragging anything makes moving forward
as difficult as men lip synching in heels.

iv.

What passes for grace.
Intervention when absolutely necessary,
a savior on a cross to save us from sin,
a reporter changing into tights in the phone booth to save distressed
   damsels,
a doctor and the word remission.

Unearned mercy.

Grace, sometimes, must be follow-through,
someone finishing the job he started.
A bullet in a chamber does not always equal mercy.
A gun to the head is something—
even if the gun isn't fired—
impossible to survive.

v.

The shininess of decay, the drumming of creation.
Breathing a habit instead of momentum,
status quo, resistance to forward motion.

vi.

Weapons are basic engineering. Mechanics of unused potential
under relegated pressure.
Controlled burn of wheat fields, contrast of power and restraint.
Kindness is a pulled trigger,
a slug propelled as it is meant to be,
an act of courage to not leave someone's life unhinged,
the cowardly thing to force someone to clean
a mess that isn't his. This cowardice we can map
on an x and y axis
if we wanted,
a proportion directly related,
shame equaling inability to remember over time.

The Florist

Once I stopped looking for an answer I came to you,
hoping that if you could not lead me back to the garden
you could at least sell me its souvenirs.

Maybe I could sit and catalogue,
write a modern pastoral,
lilacs, lilies, black-eyed susans,
hydrangeas, orchids, mountain laurel,
right here on Fifth Avenue.

I'm reading Jonah again. I place myself
in the narrative holes,

arranging myself
like baby's breath in a bouquet,
because I know the vase after the flowers die,
when you have run from God so much
that God takes his turn,
leaving nothing behind but a dead vine
in the stifling heat.

But now—gladiolas, queen anne's
lace, poppies. Anything joyful.

Remember when we stopped the car
and rushed the field of dark blue?

That day I ran but not from God.
I just ran.

Returning, we smelled the purple powder
still on our fingers.

Was it lavender, temple flowers?

No. What blooms in sand—

statice.

Resume of the Prophet

"The word of the LORD came to Jonah (dove) son of Amittai (my truth)..."
Jonah 1:1

We buried my father before his time
in late winter. His name was Truth.
The open ground drank rain before swallowing
what was left of him. The slain body of virtue.
Faint in the distance, I heard like a dove
what no one else heard,
what no one else wanted to hear.
"Get up, go.
Nineveh the wicked. Warn of destruction."

I sat in the mud and listened,
rehearsed in my head,
"In forty days this will all be dust…"

But I couldn't leave without my father—
whose starched shirts were blue with an undercurrent of blue—
all alone without a familiar voice.
The new voice grunted
like one drowning
in a puddle.
A voice wrapped in pearls.
Destruction wouldn't be the city of Nineveh,

that much I knew.
It would be mine.

I always thought I'd see my father again—
maybe in a tapestry woven with gold
or painted intricately on an Italian ceiling.

Instead of Nineveh, my mourning led me south.

Boat to Tarshish

"But Jonah ran away from the LORD and headed for Tarshish..."
Jonah 1:3

She is a vessel
shifting burdens—

uncoiling

I remember
her mouth

November in our souls

In these days
of unwelcome prophesy
the fear keeps me running

A woman carved on the bow

the only one I remember—

Jonah Descending

"From inside the fish Jonah prayed to the LORD."
Jonah 2:1

I waited for my lungs to fill with water
but I could always breathe. No gasping for breath.
Any hysterics I kept inside. Some semblance of order
had to be maintained, and in those dark hours,
when flesh that touched me was not my own,
I did not resist,
nor do I now. Some part of me
that could not have prepared for that
expected this,
standing in a doorway,
leaving hurricanes asleep in my bed.
Storms are light sleepers and I often trip down stairs.

I waited for a night unlike
others when I wanted dawn,
I waited for sand to settle
on an unknown beach with backward tides,
I waited for a final numb,
frozen and barren, to take me. Violently if necessary.
I waited for a medicine man, a shaman,
who could lay hands and know
without a sound from me my secrets.

I waited for a decade to pass.
I waited for my inner Gestapo to lay down his pistol.
I waited for dark eyes and a rain-filled kiss.
I waited to finally forget, and when that didn't happen,
I waited for a comfortable grave.

Having neither, I still breathe.

The Listening

"The word of the LORD came to Jonah a second time. 'Get up, go...'"
Jonah 3:1-2

i.

Am I why the door stands open,
why rusted hinges prevent separation?
Dare I ask such things?

After the heft of night whispered with gentle
breeze, telling me, GET UP,
GO… I listened. And with that, the concrete

parted, making crawling easier. My ribs too purple
with bruises for walking. A nurturing wind offered
strength.

Clothes torn
like a curtain
in an ancient temple.

ii.

I heard things.
The clangor, the snatch, the impact,

the click and unclick of a gun's hammer,
the forceful potential of unused cordite,
a ripping—zipper, underwear, flesh, I can't be sure—
echoing grunts and laughter,
and finally silence. Traffic maybe,
but all this is conjecture, a grasp for a complete
nightmare of memory. Fragments do me more harm than good.
I remember really only five sounds.
Laughter, ripping, click and unclick.
Silence.
Terrifying and glorious.

iii.

I became moss on the north face of a sycamore,
limbless and silent as weeds
in the garden, strangling the last of the neighbor's
St. Christopher lilies.
I am all that remains of their impatience,
the parting of legs and air,
the hush of the only thing without an echo.
Moss on any moldy doorframe.
Moss at the edge of the river.
Then I became the river.
A crescent moon waning within to a new,
which in moon terms means invisible,
nothing.
A soundless suggestion of what was.

iv.

Outside me, tightrope.
What walks walks alone. Or crawls.
Buttons loosened on a winter coat,
clasps feeble and useless.
Tea cups long shattered gathered
for a mosaic table
for brunch in the dead man's home.
Futility at every turn.
Jingles of bracelets,
the blinking of cows,
darkness of lips,
flames and carousels until the whole world,
what remains,
deafens.
There are no easy words for this.

v.

GET UP, GO…
An imperative for survival,
a call for prophesy,
an education.
If I had any other option but death
I wouldn't have moved.
If I could have compelled the world to take me
as he had,
if it could have been over for me then,
I would not have fought.
I would not have struggled.
I would not have.
I would not still.

I was still.
I waited for a conclusion,
a closure,
a final snapping shut.
I wait still.
I am not still
anymore.

vi.

A whirr, a yelp, whoosh, a thud, a sideways plunk,
a plank, the faint humming of streetlights,
rats in garbage cans,
a flicker, a spark, a rusted hinge relenting,
a whisper, a "please, please,"
knuckles scraping asphalt,
Velcro separating,
water pulsing over noodles in a strainer,
cat paws on carpet,
knitting needles rattling,
a click, a ticking watch,
a breath, a sigh, a gasp,
a scream—though I did not, that I remember well—
a chime, a ring, a chink, a ding, a ping,
a dash, a clasp, a camera click.
I pretend I heard all these things.

vii.

GET UP, GO…
"But the LORD said, 'Have you any right to be angry?'"
Jonah 4:4

The Violation and the Laughter

At 21, I chose the wrong alley
in the wrong southern city.
The barrel of the gun shone like aluminum foil,
reflecting distant street lights
and the pale fear of my temple.
The man with the gun laughed as the other took
what never occurred to me to give.
The violation or the laughter—

which was worse? What is forgiveness but a casket that will never
close? What is shame but a mirror
over a calm lake, reflections exchanged
to an unsteady infinity?

If not for the hate
would they have needed violence
to sate desires?

What is desire if not a seaweed meadow
with a lilac sky?

After, they took turns kicking
and then nothing.

I was left to crawl and bleed
out of the alley,
the belly of the whale.

My Own Midwife

"I am angry enough to die."
Jonah 4:5

The fish was convenient. Had I fled across the desert,
you would have sent hyenas to kill me
or perhaps something harder, a poisoned fruit.

Those three days I considered your call
for death. The cost for my betrayal
to become part of an underwater compost heap.

I was covered with fish vomit,
afterbirth ruining my clothes. I was never meant to die there
but be born.

And I was.
I was my own midwife,
the whale my mother.

I was spit on dry land, a puff
of smoke, a backward landslide,
the desert's prodigal disgrace.

My flesh was new, betrayed, invisibly scarred.
But I knew what had happened to it.
I understood the mutilation made by hands seen and unseen.

On land, in the alley, I had trouble walking.
Crawling hurt less.
Left foot, right foot…

but I was born something different, something darker.
You called me, tried to kill me, made me a liar to the Ninevites.
Sent a worm to destroy the only comfort you hadn't stripped,

and while I was still bleeding in the shade of the dead plant,
that night in the form of a dumpster,
I had nothing from you, kindness nor crust of bread.

Was my existence enough to justify betrayal?
Did my skin punctuate the end of your prophetic sentence?
Were my body and the life you spared testament

to your divine love and compassion? Was leaving me
with nothing but humiliation and wasted foliage
the true cause for my false prophesy?

In the dark of my womb I assembled my new body
by gathering what was left, what you hadn't gotten
your heavenly hands on, and my heart I filled
with crows, prophet birds, and in my ears
I put the sound of a thousand slaughtered
cattle. My mouth clenched on curses and
my eyes permanently emblazoned with
the barrel of a gun.

I still hear prophesies sometimes, dark premonitions
of doom and destruction,

first the fire, then the soot,

but these aren't your words.
No message of compassion and forgiveness,
some elusive divine grace.

No. My prophesies now consist of retribution.
Lilacs growing in shit.
A piñata filled with buzzards.

Your symphony
has only violins but under this din of skin
I am deaf.

Gethsemane, Kentucky

I believed that if I studied enough
I could know God. I memorized Greek paradigms
and Hebrew's guttural pictures.
That failed. I stood still
in the back garden as the bees
reclaimed what was theirs. Lilacs
released scent and inedible apples
ripened. I knew my place. I saw cardinals
taking what they wanted and leaving behind only a song
and a red feather. I looked to the ground but only saw dirt
under dirt under dirt.

Acknowledgments

"Self-Portrait as the Holy Family" first appeared in *Medulla Review 3:1*
"Cellist Writes Poems" first appeared in *PANK*
"Debris" is forthcoming in *Queer South Anthology*
"The Day I Came Out to My Parents" first appeared in *Southern Humanities Review*
"My Own Midwife" first appeared in *Borderline*
"Gethsemane, KY" first appeared in *St. Sebastian Review*

Biography

Joey Connelly received his MFA from Ashland University in 2010. He is an Assistant Professor of English at Kentucky Wesleyan College, and his work has appeared in *Louisville Review*, *New Plains Review*, *PANK*, *Southern Humanities Review,* and other publications.

Colophon

Cover font is in Book Antiqua.
Title font is in Optima.
Body text is in Perpetua.

Etchings Press

Etchings Press is a student-run publisher at the University of Indianapolis that runs a post-publication award—the Whirling Prize—as well as an annual publication contest for one poetry chapbook, one prose chapbook, and one novella.

Previous winners and publications:

Poetry
2019: *As Lovers Always Do* by Marne Wilson
2018: *In the Herald of Improbable Misfortunes* by Robert Campbell
2017: *Uncle Harold's Maxwell House Haggadah* by Danny Caine
2016: *Some Animals* by Kelli Allen
2015: *Velocity of Slugs* by Joey Connelly
2014: *Action at a Distance* by Christopher Petruccelli

Prose
2019: *Dissenting Opinion from the Committee for the Beatitudes* by Marc J. Sheehan (fiction)
2018: *The Forsaken* by Chad V. Broughman (fiction)
2017: *Unravelings* by Sarah Cheshire (essays)
2016: *Pathetic* by Shannon McLeod (essays)
2015: *Ologies* by Chelsea Biondolillo (essays)
2014: *Static: Stories* by Frederick Pelzer (fiction)

Novella
2019: *Savonne, Not Vonny* by Robin Lee Lovelace
2018: *Edge of the Known Bus Line* by James R. Gapinski
2017: *The Denialist's Almanac of American Plague and Pestilence* by Christopher Mohar
2016: *Followers* by Adam Fleming Petty

For more information, please visit etchings.uindy.edu.

www.ingramcontent.com/pod-product-compliance
Lightning Source LLC
Chambersburg PA
CBHW070442010526
44118CB00014B/2163